Family Trip

by Jamie Margaret
illustrated by Kelvin Hawley

SCHOOL PUBLISHERS

6 ©California State Railroad Museum; 8 ©Gibson Stock Photography; 11 ©Jim Yuskavitch Photography; 13 ©Kevin Levesque/Lonely Planet Images; 14 ©Seattle Photographs

Printed in the United States of America

ISBN 10: 0-15-350449-8
ISBN 13: 978-0-15-350449-5

Ordering Options
ISBN 10: 0-15-350332-7 (Grade 2 Below-Level Collection)
ISBN 13: 978-0-15-350332-0 (Grade 2 Below-Level Collection)
ISBN 10: 0-15-357459-3 (package of 5)
ISBN 13: 978-0-15-357459-7 (package of 5)

1 2 3 4 5 6 7 8 9 10   179   15 14 13 12 11 10 09 08 07 06

Characters

Mom

Janie

Grandma

Dad

Aidan

Grandpa

SCENE ONE

Setting: The family's home in San Francisco, California

Mom: Come on, everyone. Let's go on our family trip!

Dad: Yes! We need to get going without delay. There is no time to spare!

Janie: All the bags are in the car.

Aidan: Hooray! Let's drive to Seattle, Washington.

Grandma: This will be a fantastic trip!

Grandpa: I'm sure I'll get lots of impressive picture. Smile everyone!

SCENE TWO

Setting: California State Railroad Museum in Sacramento, California

Grandpa: This place is so historical. I like the collection of old trains and the rare photos.

Grandma: Trains were once the fastest way to get around.

Mom: Yes, trains were used to take food supplies all around the country.

Dad: More people settled in California after the discovery of gold. The trains became very busy.

Janie: Look, here comes the steam train.

Aidan: Hooray! Let's go on the train.

SCENE THREE

Setting: Lake Red Bluff Recreational Area in Red Bluff, California

Mom: What a grand lake!

Janie: Let's go swimming.

Aidan: Oh, yes! Let's go!

Mom: I'm coming, too!

Grandma: I'm going bird-watching. I could see a majestic golden eagle!

Grandpa: Here are the fishing rods.

Dad: Grandpa and I are going fishing. We might catch our dinner!

SCENE FOUR

Setting: Oregon Caves National Monument in Cave Junction, Oregon

Aidan: These caves are great.

Dad: A man found them when he was chasing after his dog. The dog was running after a bear.

Mom: A bear?

Janie: It is very narrow here.

Grandma: Yes, it is. Walk carefully so you don't touch the walls.

Janie: Can we touch the walls gently?

Grandpa: You shouldn't because the oil from your skin could damage the rock.

Mom: I'm glad I brought my sweater. It's very cold in here.

SCENE FIVE

Setting: Pike Place Market in Seattle, Washington

Janie: This market is a very upbeat place.

Grandma: Look at these fantastic flowers. They are so fragrant.

Mom: I can see some lovely fruit just beyond the flowers.

Dad: We can get our entire lunch here.

Aidan: Can we have our lunch at a park?

Grandpa: That is a great idea! I saw a park on the way here.

Janie: I can't wait to explore all of Seattle.

All: What a great family trip!

Think Critically

1. What happened when gold was discovered in California?

2. What type of bird did Grandma think she might see at the recreational area?

3. Why do you think it was very cold in the caves?

4. What tells you that this story is a Readers' Theater?

5. Would you like to visit a cave? Why or why not?

 **Social Studies**

Write a Paragraph The family visits a market. Write a paragraph telling why some sellers might sell things at a market.

School-Home Connection Tell a family member about the story. Then talk about places you would like to visit on a family vacation.